HMH  into **Math**™

Getting Ready for High-Stakes Assessment

Grade 1

Contents

About *Getting Ready for High-Stakes Assessment* . . . . **v**

Assessment Item Types . . . . **vi**

Standards Practice

Use Addition and Subtraction Within 20 to Solve Word Problems **1**

Add Three Whole Numbers Whose Sum is Less Than or Equal to 20 . . . . **3**

Apply Properties of Operations as Strategies to Add and Subtract **5**

Understand Subtraction as an Unknown-Addend Problem **7**

Relate Counting to Addition and Subtraction **9**

Add and Subtract Within 20 . . . . **11**

Understand the Meaning of the Equal Sign. **13**

Determine the Unknown Number in an Addition or Subtraction Equation **15**

Count to 120, Starting at Any Number Less Than 120 . . . . **17**

Understand that the Digits of a Two-Digit Number Represent Tens and Ones **19**

Understand that 10 can be Thought of as a Bundle of Ten Ones **21**

Understand that Numbers From 11 to 19 are Composed of a Ten and Some Ones **23**

Understand that Some Numbers Refer to a Certain Number of Tens **25**

Compare Two Two-Digit Numbers **27**

Add Within 100 . . . . **29**

Mentally Find 10 More or 10 Less Than a Given Two-Digit Number **31**

Subtract Multiples of 10 From Multiples of 10 in the Range 10–90 . . . . **33**

Order and Compare Objects by Length **35**

Explore Length as a Whole Number of Length Units **37**

© Houghton Mifflin Harcourt Publishing Company

Tell and Write Time in Hours and Half-Hours **39**

Organize, Represent, and Interpret Data **41**

Distinguish Between Attributes, and Build and Draw Shapes **43**

Compose 2-D or 3-D Shapes to Create a Composite Shape **45**

Partition Shapes Into Equal Shares, and Describe the Shares **47**

Individual Record Form **49**

Practice Test 1 . . . . **51**

Practice Test 2 . . . . **59**

Practice Test 3 . . . . **67**

About *Getting Ready for High-Stakes Assessment*

This *Getting Ready for High-Stakes Assessment* print guide consists of standards-based practice and practice tests.

Standards-Based Practice

The items in each practice set are designed to give students exposure to the wide variety of ways in which a standard may be assessed.

All standards-based practice sets are available to students online. Online item types include traditional multiple choice as well as technology-enhanced item types. The online practice experience also offers students hints, corrective feedback, and opportunities to try an item multiple times. You can assign online standards-based practice and receive instant access to student data and reports. The reports can help you pinpoint student strengths and weaknesses and tailor instruction to meet their needs. The standards-based practice sets in this guide mirror those found online; however, some technology-enhanced item types have been modified or replaced with items suitable for paper-and-pencil testing.

Practice Tests

Into Math also includes three practice tests designed to simulate high-stakes testing experiences similar to ones that students will encounter in the upper elementary grades. The practice tests are available online. Online item types include traditional multiple choice as well as technology-enhanced item types. You can assign the online tests for instant access to data and standards alignments. The practice tests in this guide mirror those found online; however, some technology-enhanced item types were modified or replaced with items suitable for paper-and-pencil testing. This guide includes record forms for these tests that show the content focus and depth of knowledge for each item.

Assessment Item Types

The high-stakes assessments students will take in the upper elementary grades contain item types beyond the traditional multiple-choice format. This allows for a more robust assessment of students' understanding of concepts and skills. High-stakes assessments are administered via computers, and *Into Math* presents items in formats similar to what students will see on the real tests. The following information is provided to help you familiarize your students with these different types of items. An example of each item type appears on the following pages. You may want to use the examples to introduce the item types to students. These pages describe the most common item types. You may find other types on some tests.

Example 1: Multiselect

Upon first glance, many students may easily confuse this item type with a traditional multiple-choice item. Explain to students that this type of item will have a special direction line that asks them to choose all the answers to the problem that are correct.

Which numbers are less than 25?

Choose the **2** correct answers.

○ 32   ○ 52

○ 24   ○ 17

Example 2: Fill in the Blank

Sometimes when students take a digital test, they will have to select a word, number, or symbol from a drop-down list or drag answer options into blanks. The print versions of the *Into Math* tests ask students to write the correct answer in the blank.

Ali puts 5 books in his bag. He puts 7 more books in his bag. How can Ali find the number of books in his bag?

Fill in the blanks with the correct numbers from the list to create an equation Ali could use.

_____   _____   _____

- - - - - - + - - - - - - = - - - - - - -

_____   _____   _____

| 2   5   7   12 |

Example 3: Classification

Some *Into Math* assessment items require students to categorize numbers or shapes. Digital versions of this item type require students to drag answer options into the correct place in a table. When the classification involves more complex equations or drawings, each object will have a letter next to it. Print versions of this item type will ask students to write answer options in the correct place in the table. Tell students that sometimes they may write the same number or word in more than one column of the table.

Write the numbers in the correct place in the table to show if they are greater than 31 or less than 31.

Greater than 31	Less than 31

47   33   29   89

Example 4: Matching

In some items, students will need to match one set of objects to another. In some computer-based items, students will need to drag an answer option into a box next to the element it matches. On paper-based tests, they do this by drawing a line connecting the two elements that match.

Draw a line to match each model with an equation. You will not use all the equations.

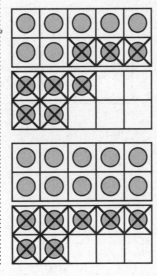

$$15 - 8 = 7$$

$$12 - 3 = 9$$

$$17 - 7 = 10$$

Example 5: Hotspot

Students may need to answer questions by interacting with a piece of art. On the digital tests, certain regions of the art are designated as "hot," meaning that students are able to click on them. Students click on the correct region or regions of the art to answer the question. On paper-based tests, students circle the correct region or regions of the art to answer the question.

Circle the **2** groups of coins that show 15 cents.

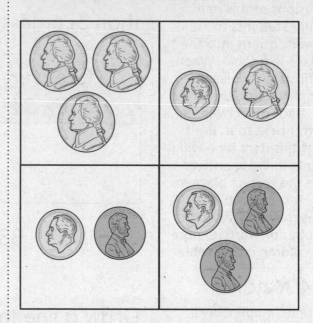

Example 6: Shading

Shading items allow students to select boxes to shade portions of an interactive rectangular array. In the print versions of these items, students shade a model to show the relationship being assessed.

Shade a fourth of the model.

1 Sam counted 4 worms. Jen counted 2 worms. What equation can be used to show how many worms they counted?

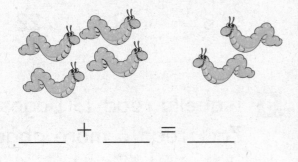

___ + ___ = ___

2 Taylor has 4 red leaves and 4 yellow leaves. How many leaves does Taylor have altogether?

_____ leaves

3 James has 5 marbles. He finds more marbles. Now he has 9 marbles. How many marbles does James find?

Write the correct number in the box in the bar model.

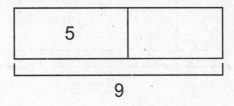

4 There are 8 bugs on a flower. The 3 biggest bugs fly away. How many bugs are on the flower now?

○ 2   ○ 5   ○ 6

5 Ms. Clark put 8 cows in her barn. There are 2 brown cows. The other cows are white. How many cows are white?

Write the correct number in the bar model.

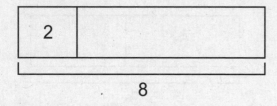

6 Jake has 16 pencils. He gives away some. Now he has 9 pencils. How many pencils does Jake give away?

_____ pencils

7 Maisy picks 15 flowers. She picks 7 pink flowers and the rest are yellow. How many yellow flowers does Maisy pick?

○ 8   ○ 9   ○ 22

8 Isabella read 13 pages. Zack read 6 more pages than Isabella. How many pages did Zack read?

○ 7   ○ 18   ○ 19

9 There were 12 ducks swimming in a pond. There were 5 ducks sitting in the grass. How many fewer ducks were sitting in the grass?

○ 6   ○ 7   ○ 18

10 Cade has 14 toy cars. Travis has 3 toy cars. How many toy cars do the boys have altogether?

○ 11   ○ 17   ○ 19

1 Beth sees 4 red birds. She sees 2 yellow birds and 4 blue birds. Which equation shows how to find how many birds Beth sees?

○ $4 + 2 = 6$

○ $4 + 2 + 2 = 8$

○ $4 + 2 + 4 = 10$

2 David has 6 red markers, 5 green markers, and 7 blue markers. How many markers does David have in all?

David has _____ markers.

3 Enzo won 5 games. Emily won 4 more games than Enzo. Which model shows how many games Enzo and Emily won?

○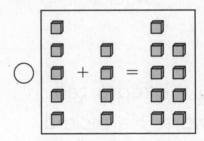

○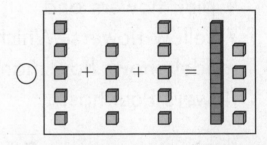

○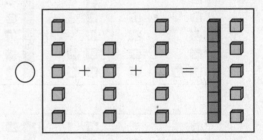

4 Ted has 7 red apples. He has 3 yellow apples and 2 green apples. Which equation shows how to find how many apples Ted has?

○ $7 + 3 + 2 = 11$

○ $7 + 3 + 2 = 12$

○ $7 + 3 + 2 = 13$

Name _____

5 Judy put 8 green blocks, 4 red blocks, and 2 green blocks in a box. How many blocks did Judy put in the box?

_____ blocks

6 Paul picked 6 red flowers. He picked 4 pink flowers and 7 yellow flowers. Which model shows how many flowers Paul has?

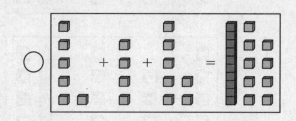

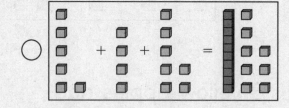

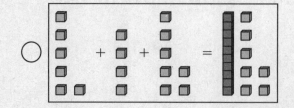

7 Kyle saw 3 big frogs at the lake. He saw 2 more little frogs than big frogs. How many frogs did Kyle see?

_____

8 A squirrel put 6 little acorns and 3 big acorns in his nest. He put 1 more little acorn in his nest. How many acorns did the squirrel put in his nest?

○ 9
○ 10
○ 14

9 Joey has 6 blue marbles. He has 3 red marbles and 5 green marbles. How many marbles does Joey have?

_____ marbles

1 What number is missing from the equation
5 = 5 + ☐ ?

⃝ 1   ⃝ 0   ⃝ 5

2 Draw a line from each equation to the box with the
equation that means the same. You will not use all the
equations.

3 + 6 = ☐ •   • 3 + 4 = ☐

                          • 4 + 2 = ☐

2 + 4 = ☐ •   • 4 + 4 = ☐

4 + 3 = ☐ •   • 6 + 3 = ☐

3 Write the missing
number in the equation.

9 + 10 = 10 + _____

4 Write the missing
number in each
equation.

_____ + 5 = 7

5 + _____ = 7

5 Look at the row of cubes.

One way to add the
cubes is 3 + 6 + 2 = 11.

Write the correct
numbers in the boxes to
show another way to add
the cubes.

3 + _____ = _____

6 What is another way to add 3 + 7 + 2?

○ 3 + 7   ○ 3 + 8   ○ 10 + 2

---

7 Which equations mean the same?

Draw a line from each addition equation to an equation that means the same. You will use all the equations.

| 9 + 3 + 2 = ☐ | ● | ● | 9 + 10 = ☐ |

| 9 + 3 + 7 = ☐ | ● | ● | 9 + 5 = ☐ |

| 9 + 4 + 3 = ☐ | ● | ● | 9 + 7 = ☐ |

---

8 Which of these means the same as 4 + 6?

○ 3 + 6   ○ 4 + 5   ○ 6 + 4

---

9 Clark has 7 old pencils and 3 new pencils. Which equation could he use to find the number of pencils?

○ 7 + 2 = 9   ○ 3 + 7 = 10   ○ 3 + 6 = 10

---

10 Which shows a way to add 4 + 5 + 2?

○ 4 + 6 = 10   ○ 8 + 2 = 10   ○ 9 + 2 = 11

1 Which addition fact can help solve $13 - 4$?

○ $7 + 6 = 13$
○ $6 + 8 = 14$
○ $4 + 9 = 13$

2 What number is missing from both of these equations?

$7 + \boxed{} = 15$

$15 - 7 = \boxed{}$

○ 6
○ 7
○ 8

3 Which addition fact can help you solve $18 - 7$?

○ $3 + 4 = 7$
○ $7 + 4 = 11$
○ $11 + 7 = 18$

4 What is a subtraction fact you can solve by using the addition fact $3 + 1 = 4$?

___ $-$ ___ $=$ ___

5 Which addition fact can help you solve $16 - 9$?

○ $9 + 7 = 16$
○ $9 + 8 = 17$
○ $16 + 9 = 25$

6 What number is missing from the equations?

$15 - 9 = $ _____

$9 + $ _____ $= 15$

Name _____

7 What number correctly
completes the number
sentences?

$$14 - 5 = \boxed{}$$

$$\boxed{} + 5 = 14$$

○ 7

○ 8

○ 9

8 What is an addition
sentence that will help
solve $9 - 4$?

___ + ___ = ___

9 Write a subtraction
equation you can solve
by using $4 + 2 = 6$.

___ − ___ = ___

10 What is an addition fact
that can help you solve
$8 - 2$?

___ + ___ = ___

8

1 Count on from 5.

5 + 3 = ?

What is the number that is 3 more?

○ 7
○ 8
○ 9

2 Count on from 6.

What is the number that shows 2 more?

_____

3 Count back. What is the number that is 1 less?

6 − 1 = _____

4 Isaac had 10 pencils. He gave away 2. How should Isaac count to find how many pencils he has left?

○ 10, 9
○ 10, 9, 8
○ 10, 11, 12

5 How many should you count on to find the missing number in each equation?

Draw a line to match each equation to the correct answer. You will use all the answers.

| 6 + ? = 8 | ● | ● | Count on 1. |

| 3 + ? = 6 | ● | ● | Count on 2. |

| 10 + ? = 11 | ● | ● | Count on 3. |

Name _____

6 Count on.

15 + 3 = ?

What is the sum?

○ 18   ○ 17   ○ 16

7 Show how to use counting to add 14 + 2.

Fill in the blanks with the correct numbers.

14, _____, _____

8 Kim has 14 strawberries. She eats 3. How should Kim count to find how many strawberries she has left?

○ 14, 13, 12   ○ 14, 13, 12, 11   ○ 14, 15, 16, 17

9 How many should you count back to find the missing number in each equation?

Draw lines from the correct answer to each equation. You will use all the answers.

11 − ? = 8	●	●	Count back 1.
7 − ? = 6	●	●	Count back 2.
9 − ? = 7	●	●	Count back 3.

10 Count back.

4 − 1 = ?

○ 2   ○ 3   ○ 5

1 Which shows how to make a ten to solve 15 − 6?

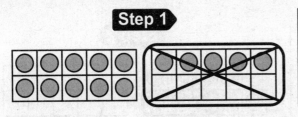 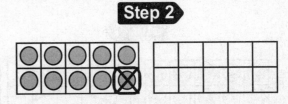

○ 10 − 1   ○ 10 − 5 − 1   ○ 15 − 5 − 1

2 What is a *count on 2* fact that has a sum of 6?

2 + _____ = 6

3 Which doubles fact can be used to solve 5 + 4?

○ 6 + 6 = 12
○ 4 + 4 = 8
○ 3 + 3 = 6

4 The model shows 9 + 2 = 11.

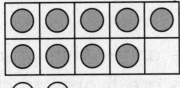

What is the 10 fact that has the same sum?

10 + _____ = _____

5 Which shows a way to make a ten to solve 9 + 7?

○ 9 + 1 + 6   ○ 9 + 2 + 6   ○ 9 + 10 + 7

Name _____

6 How does the model show 14 − 7?

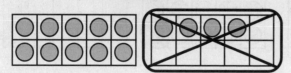

Step 1: 14 − _____ = 10

Step 2: 10 − _____ = 7

7 Which equation shows a way to find 13 − 6?

○ 13 − 3 = ☐

○ 10 − 3 − 3 = ☐☐

○ 13 − 3 − 3 = ☐☐

8 Tina has a book. She reads 10 pages. Then she reads 6 more pages.

I know Tina reads _____ pages because _____ − 6 = 10.

9 Which doubles fact helps you solve 8 + 9?

○ 6 + 6 = 12

○ 7 + 7 = 14

○ 8 + 8 = 16

10 There are 4 white trucks. There are 5 gray trucks. How many trucks are there in all?

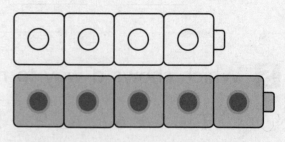

4 + 4 + _____ = _____

© Houghton Mifflin Harcourt Publishing Company

1 Which number makes the equation true?

$$11 - 2 = 6 + \boxed{}$$

○ 3　　　　○ 4　　　　○ 6

---

2 Place an X in the table to show if each equation is true or false.

	True	False
1 + 9 = 9 − 1		
8 + 1 = 2 + 7		
19 = 19		

---

3 Which equation is true?

○ 9 = 6 + 2
○ 7 + 2 = 9 + 1
○ 5 + 4 = 4 + 5

---

4 Place an X in the table to show if each equation is true or false.

	True	False
9 + 7 = 16		
16 − 9 = 9 + 7		
9 − 7 = 7 + 9		

Name _____

5 Which number makes the equation true?

$$5 + 4 = 10 - \square$$

○ 3   ○ 2   ○ 1

6 Place an X in the table to show if each equation is true or false.

	True	False
$12 - 3 = 9 - 0$		
$11 - 1 = 5 + 5 + 1$		
$10 = 8 - 2$		

7 Which equation is false?

○ $10 + 0 = 6 + 4$
○ $6 + 3 = 3 + 6$
○ $5 + 2 = 5 - 2$

8 Place an X in the table to show if each equation is true or false.

	True	False
$5 - 4 = 4 - 3$		
$13 = 6 + 6 + 1$		
$6 + 2 = 2 + 8$		

14

1 Use this model to find the missing numbers in these equations.

$7 +$ _____ $= 12$

$12 - 7 =$ _____

2 What number will make all of these equations true?

$? + 3 = 11$

$3 + ? = 11$

$11 - 3 = ?$

$11 - ? = 3$

○ 3   ○ 8   ○ 9

3 What number is missing from both of these equations?

$14 -$ _____ $= 9$ $9 +$ _____ $= 14$

4 Use this model to find the missing number in these equations.

$6 +$ _____ $= 16$ $16 - 6 =$ _____

5 What number is missing from this equation?

$$\boxed{} + 2 = 7$$

○ 4 　　○ 5 　　○ 6

---

6 What number is missing from this equation?

$$8 - \boxed{} = 6$$

○ 4 　　○ 3 　　○ 2

---

7 Maria needs 1 plate to go with each cup. She has 3 plates and 5 cups.

How many more plates does Maria need?

$$3 + \underline{} = 5$$

---

8 What number is missing from this equation?

$$6 - \boxed{} = 6$$

○ 0 　　○ 1 　　○ 6

---

9 Which is the missing number in these related facts?

$$? + 4 = 13$$

$$4 + ? = 13$$

$$13 - 4 = ?$$

$$13 - ? = 4$$

○ 7

○ 8

○ 9

---

10 What number is missing from both of these equations?

$$\boxed{} - 5 = 5$$

$$5 + 5 = \boxed{}$$

○ 5

○ 10

○ 12

1 Carrie is counting her pennies like this.

28, 29, _____, 31, 32, 33, 34

What number is missing?

○ 3
○ 13
○ 30

2 How many circles are in this model?

○ 21
○ 25
○ 26

3 Lucy counts 39 cubes. Then she counts forward 3 more cubes. Show how she counts.

38, 39, _____, _____, _____

4 What number comes next? Draw lines from each number to the number that comes next. You will not use all the numbers.

28 ●	● 16
69 ●	● 29
15 ●	● 55
	● 70

5 Count by ones. What 3 numbers come next?

109, 110, 111, _____, _____, _____

Name _____

6 How many squares are here?

_____

7 Felix is counting by ones like this: 46, 47, 48, 49. What number should Felix count next?

46, 47, 48, 49, _____

_____

8 Count by ones.

101, 102, 103, _____, 105, 106

What number is missing?

○ 14
○ 100
○ 104

9 What number does the model show?

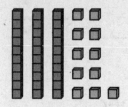

○ 31
○ 41
○ 51

_____

10 What number comes next? Draw lines from each number to the number that comes next. You will not use all the numbers.

35	●	●	69
59	●	●	66
65	●	●	60
		●	36

1 What does the model show?

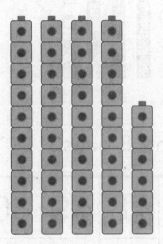

- ○ 4 + 6 = 10
- ○ 40 + 6 = 46
- ○ 60 + 4 = 64

2 Mika has 3 whole packs of markers and 9 loose markers. Each pack of markers contains 10 markers. How many markers does Mika have in all?

Fill in the blank with the correct number.

_____ markers

3 Fill in the blank with the correct number. You will not use all the numbers.

There are _____ tens and _____ ones in 73.

| 3 | 7 | 30 |

4 What does the model show?

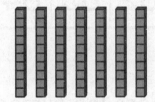

- ○ 6 ones
- ○ 6 tens and 0 ones
- ○ 0 tens

5 Marja and Sam go apple picking. They fill 6 bags with 10 apples in each bag and have 8 more apples. How many apples did they pick?

- ○ 14   ○ 68   ○ 86

Name _____

6 Which model shows 34?

○   ○ 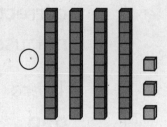   ○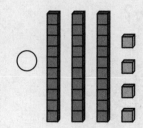

7 Circle the number that shows 7 tens and 8 ones.

71	72	73	74	75	76	77	78	79	80
81	82	83	84	85	86	87	88	89	90

8 What does the number 52 represent?

○ 5 ones and 2 ones
○ 5 ones and 2 tens
○ 5 tens and 2 ones

9 How many tens are in 75?

○ 7
○ 5
○ 12

1 What number does this model show?

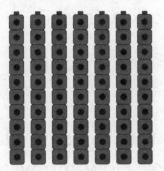

- ○ 7 ones = 70 tens
- ○ 7 ones = 70 ones
- ○ 7 tens = 70 ones

2 How many frogs are in the picture?

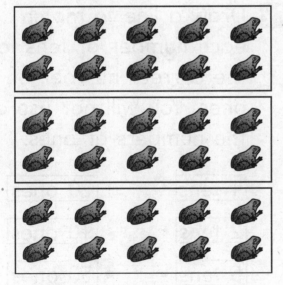

_____

3 What number does the quick picture show?

_____

4 What number does this model show?

○ 3 ones   ○ 3   ○ 3 tens

_____

5 How many acorns are in the picture?

_____

6 Paul has 50 stickers. He puts them in groups of 10. How many groups of 10 can Paul make?

○ 5
○ 6
○ 7

7 Which of these is true?

○ 10 tens = 10
○ 10 ones = 1 ten
○ 10 tens = 1 one

8 Sally has 90 marbles. How many sets of 10 marbles can she make?

○ 0
○ 9
○ 10

9 Fill in the blank with the correct number to make the equation true.

_____ tens = 60 ones

10 Fill in the blank with the correct number to make the equation true.

8 tens = _____ ones

11 Mary is making sets of 10 blocks. How many blocks does she need to make 2 sets of 10?

○ 2
○ 12
○ 20

12 Draw a line to match each number of tens to the correct number of ones. You will not use all the numbers of ones.

4 tens	•	•	20 ones
2 tens	•	•	40 ones
5 tens	•	•	50 ones
		•	5 ones

1 What does this model show?

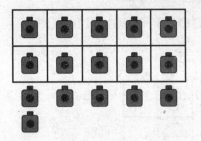

○ 10 + 1 = 11
○ 10 + 5 = 15
○ 10 + 6 = 16

2 Fill in the blanks with the correct numbers.

There are _____ ten and _____ ones in 15.

3 Matthew has 1 box of 10 crayons. He has 9 more crayons on his desk. How many crayons does Matthew have?

_____ crayons

4 Fill in the blanks with the correct numbers.

There are _____ ten and _____ ones in 12.

5 How many markers are shown?

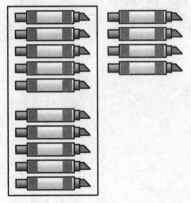

_____

6 What does this model show?

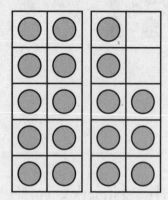

○ 10 + 3 = 13

○ 10 + 7 = 17

○ 10 + 8 = 18

7 What is true about the number 13?

There are _____ ten and _____ ones in 13.

8 What does this model show?

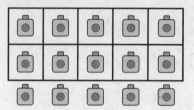

_____ ten and

_____ ones = _____

9 What does this model show?

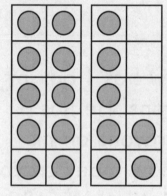

○ 1 ten and 7 ones = 17

○ 1 one and 7 tens = 17

○ 1 ten and 7 ones = 71

10 1 ten + 1 one = _____

1 What number is missing?

3 tens = _____

2 What does this model show?

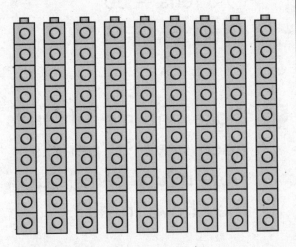

○ 9
○ 80
○ 90

3 Which of these is true?

○ 0 tens + 5 ones = 50
○ 5 tens + 0 ones = 5
○ 5 tens + 0 ones = 50

4 Dan has 6 plates of cookies. He puts 10 cookies on each plate. He counts the cookies like this.

10, 20, _____,

40, 50, _____

What numbers are missing?

○ 3 and 6
○ 30 and 60
○ 30 and 70

5 What does this model show?

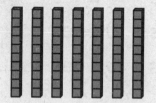

_____ tens +

_____ ones = _____

6 Rosa has 80 shells. She puts all her shells in rows of 10 each. How many rows of shells can Rosa make?

_____ rows of shells

7 2 tens + 2 tens = ▢

○ 4

○ 20

○ 40

8 What does this model show?

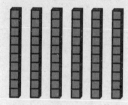

○ 6 tens = 6

○ 6 tens = 60

○ 60 tens = 6

9 Blake and his 3 friends each have 10 pencils. How many pencils do they have in all?

_____ tens = _____

10 What is the missing number in the equation?

1 ten + 0 ones = _____

1 Which of these is true about 71 and 35?

○ 71 is less than 35.

○ 71 is equal to 35.

○ 71 is greater than 35.

2 Draw a line from each number to show if it is less than 51 or greater than 51. You will use all the numbers.

Less than 51	•		• 41
			• 48
			• 75
Greater than 51	•		• 37

3 Which symbol belongs in the box?

28 ☐ 24

○ >   ○ <   ○ =

4 Draw a line from each number to show if it is less than 63 or greater than 63. You will use all the numbers.

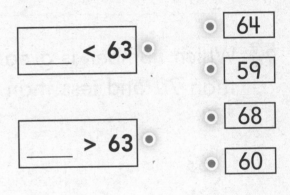

_____ < 63 •   • 64

• 59

_____ > 63 •   • 68

• 60

5 Circle all the number sentences that are true.

27 > 31

35 = 35

71 < 77

82 < 70

Name _____

6 Which symbol makes this number sentence true: <, =, or >?

46 _____ 58

_____

7 Which number is greater than 70 and less than 73?

○ 63

○ 71

○ 74

_____

8 Which is true?

○ 54 < 58

○ 54 > 58

○ 54 = 58

9 What number will make both of these number sentences true?

▣ < 58

▣ > 56

_____

_____

10 Which is true?

○ 46 < 46

○ 46 = 46

○ 46 > 46

1 What is 30 + 40?

○ 34
○ 70
○ 80

2 Marta drew a model of an addition problem.

What does the model show?

Circle the **2** correct answers.

20 + 7

20 + 70

2 tens + 7 tens

3 Gina has 14 pennies. Her brother gives her 20 more pennies. How many pennies does Gina have now?

○ 16
○ 34
○ 70

4 What is 36 + 6?

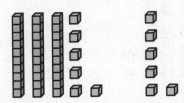

36 + 6 = _____

5 What is the sum?

$$\begin{array}{r} 57 \\ +3 \\ \hline \\ \hline \end{array}$$

Name _____

6 What is the sum?

$$\begin{array}{r} 45 \\ +3 \\ \hline \end{array}$$

- ○ 48
- ○ 75
- ○ 84

7 The model shows a way to add 47 + 6.

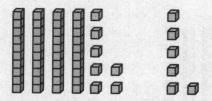

What is another way to add 47 + 6?

50 + _____ = _____

8 What is the sum?

$$\begin{array}{r} 26 \\ +5 \\ \hline \end{array}$$

- ○ 30
- ○ 31
- ○ 76

9 How many tens and ones are in the sum of 60 + 30?

- ○ 6 tens and 3 ones
- ○ 9 tens and 0 ones
- ○ 90 tens and 0 ones

10 Write the addition sentence that the model shows.

Tens	Ones

+

_____ + _____ = _____

1 Look at this model of a number.

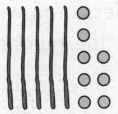

Which model shows a number that is 10 less?

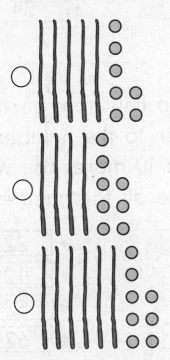

2 What number is 10 less than 47?

○ 37
○ 46
○ 57

3 Look at this model of a number.

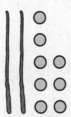

Which model shows a number that is 10 more?

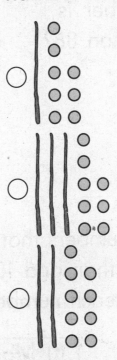

4 Jill has 35 pennies. Paul has 10 more pennies than Jill. How many pennies does Paul have?

○ 25
○ 45
○ 46

Name _____

5 What numbers are 10 more than and 10 less than 70?

10 more than 70 is _____.

10 less than 70 is _____.

6 What number is 10 more than 88?

○ 78
○ 89
○ 98

7 Write the numbers that are 10 less than and 10 more than each number.

10 Less		10 More
	22	
	45	55

8 What numbers are 10 more than and 10 less than 80?

10 more than 80 is _____.

10 less than 80 is _____.

9 Draw a line from each number to the number that is 10 less. You will not use all the numbers.

54	•	•	24
34	•	•	34
		•	44
64	•	•	54

10 Draw a line from each number to the number that is 10 more. You will not use all the numbers.

52	•	•	22
42	•	•	42
		•	52
32	•	•	62

1 What subtraction sentence does this model show?

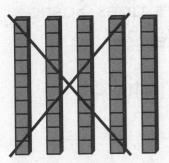

The model shows that

_____ – _____ =

_____.

2 What is the difference?

$50 - 20 = \square$

○ 20
○ 30
○ 70

---

3 Draw lines from each addition equation to the box containing the subtraction equation it helps solve. You will use all the addition equations.

| 60 − 40 = ? | • | • | 60 + 30 = 90 |

| 90 − 30 = ? | • | • | 20 + 40 = 60 |

| 70 − 50 = ? | • | • | 20 + 50 = 70 |

Name _____

4 Karla has 80 cents. She spends 20 cents. How much money does Karla have left?

○ 40 cents
○ 50 cents
○ 60 cents

5 Mr. Jones has 90 pencils. He sells 40 of the pencils. How many pencils does Mr. Jones have left?

_____ pencils

6 What is the difference?

$$\begin{array}{r} 60 \\ -30 \\ \hline \end{array}$$

○ 30
○ 40
○ 90

7 Sasha has 70 stickers. She uses 40 of the stickers. How many stickers does Sasha have left?

_____ stickers

8 Which equation shows how to find $40 - 30$?

○ 4 tens − 3 tens = 1 ten
○ 4 tens − 3 ones = 1 one
○ 4 tens − 3 tens = 7 tens

9 What is the difference?

$$\begin{array}{r} 80 \\ -50 \\ \hline \end{array}$$

○ 30
○ 40
○ 50

1 Number the pictures in order from 1 for the shortest to 3 for the longest.

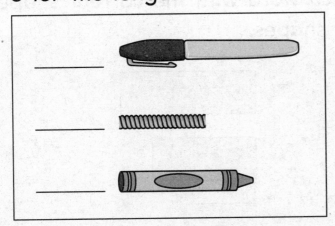

---

2 Which picture shows the shortest line on the top?

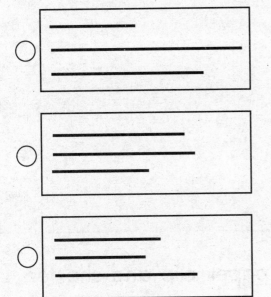

3 Which shows the leaves in order from longest on the top to shortest on the bottom?

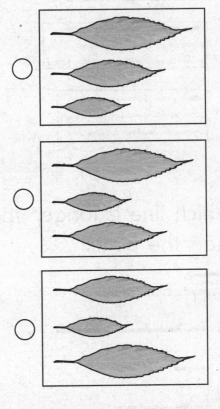

Name _____

4 Which are shortest and longest?

Draw lines to match each word with the correct shape.
You will not use all the shapes.

| shortest | ● | ● | 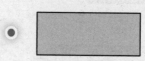 |

| longest | ● | ● | |

| | | ● | |

---

5 Which picture shows the last line being the longest?

○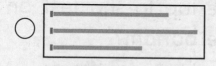

○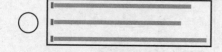

○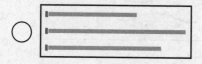

---

6 Which line is longer than the paper clip and shorter than the pencil?

○ ──────────────

○ ────

○ ─────────

36

Name _____

1 How many paper clips long is the toy car?

- ○ 1 paper clip
- ○ 4 paper clips
- ○ 6 paper clips

2 How many pennies long is the caterpillar?

Fill in the blank with the correct number.

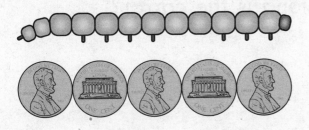

_____ pennies

3 How many paper clips long is the pencil?

○ 1 paper clip   ○ 3 paper clips   ○ 8 paper clips

Name _____

4 How many beads long is the ribbon?

○ 6

○ 7

○ 8

5 Mina has a marker that is longer than the eraser. The marker is shorter than her pencil. How many paper clips long could the marker be?

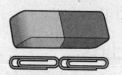

○ 6 paper clips

○ 3 paper clips

○ 1 paper clip

6 About how many pennies long is the carrot?

○ 4 pennies

○ 5 pennies

○ 8 pennies

Name _____

1 Look at the hour hand on this clock.

Which of these could be the correct time?

○ 2:00
○ 3:00
○ 4:00

2 Which number should the minute hand point to on the clock to show 3:00?

The minute hand of the clock should point to the _____.

3 What time does this clock show?

○ 8 o'clock
○ half past 9:00
○ half past 8:00

4 What time does this clock show?

○ 2:30
○ 3:00
○ 3:30

Name _____

5 Look at this clock.

Which of these clocks shows the same time?

○ 5:00

○ 5:30

○ 12:00

6 What number should the minute hand point to on the clock to show 9:30?

7 Look at this clock.

Which of these clocks shows the same time?

○

○

○

8 What time does this clock show?

○ 1:30   ○ 6:30   ○ 12:30

1 Look at this graph about pets.

Pets We Have						
🐕 dog	⚲	⚲	⚲	⚲	⚲	⚲
🐈 cat	⚲	⚲	⚲	⚲	⚲	
🐹 hamster	⚲	⚲				

Each ⚲ stands for 1 child.

Part A
How many children have a cat?

_____

Part B
How many more children have dogs than cats?

○ 1
○ 6
○ 11

2 This graph shows how many toys are at the store.

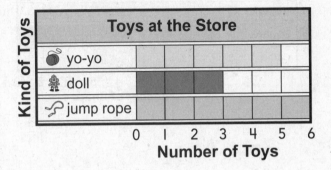

Part A
How many jump ropes does the store have?

_____

Part B
The store sells 2 dolls. How many dolls does the store have now?

○ 1
○ 3
○ 4

Name _____

3 Look at the graph about shapes in a box.

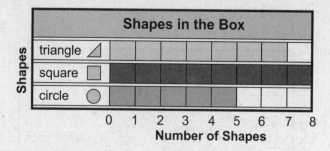

Shapes in the Box

Shapes	0	1	2	3	4	5	6	7	8
triangle △									
square ▢									
circle ◯									

Number of Shapes

Part A
What is true about the numbers of triangles, squares, and circles in the box?

There are _____ more squares than circles in the box.

The number of circles is _____ less than the number of triangles.

Part B
Write an equation that shows how many shapes are in the box.

7 + ___ + ___ = ___

4 Some children made this chart to show which fruit they like best.

Fruit We Like Best	
🍎	Жⵏ
🍐	‖
🍌	Ж ‖

Part A
Which fruit do most children like best?

◯ apples
◯ pears
◯ bananas

Part B
How many children chose each kind of fruit?

_____ chose apples.

_____ chose pears.

_____ chose bananas.

Name _____

1 Circle each shape that has both flat and curved surfaces.

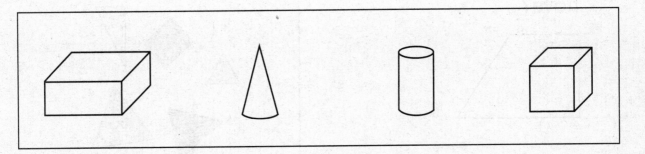

2 Billy is drawing a hexagon. How many straight sides should Billy draw?

○ 4
○ 5
○ 6

3 How many surfaces of this  are shaped like a circle?

_____

4 Which of these has a surface shaped like a rectangle?

○

○

○

© Houghton Mifflin Harcourt Publishing Company

Grade 1 • Standards-Based Practice

Name _____

5 How many vertices (corners) does this shape have?

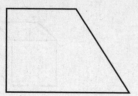

_____

6 Which shape has a curved surface and no flat surfaces?

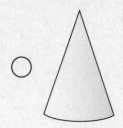

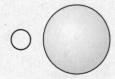

7 How many of these shapes are triangles?

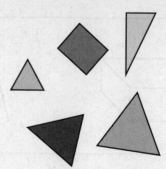

_____

8 Mary began drawing this rectangle.

How many more sides should Mary draw to finish her rectangle?

○ 2
○ 3
○ 4

_____

9 How many flat surfaces does a cube have?

_____

44

1 Which new shapes can be made
by combining these two shapes?
Circle the **2** correct shapes.

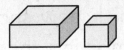

---

2 Eve made this big shape
by combining some
shapes. How many
and [rectangular prism] did Eve use?

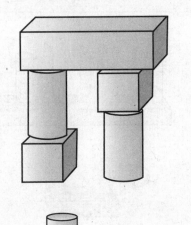

_____ [cylinder]

_____ [rectangular prism]

3 Which set of small
shapes could be
combined to make this
new big shape?

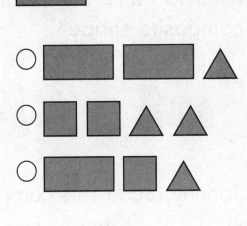

Name _____

4 Which new shape was made by combining these two shapes?

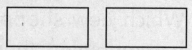

○ 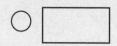   ○    ○

5 This new shape was made by putting together 2 shapes. One shape was a triangle. What was the other shape? Circle the correct shape.

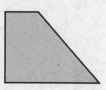

6 Which composite shape was used to make this combined composite shape?

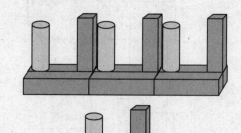

○ 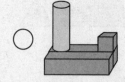   ○ 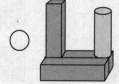   ○

7 Johnny made this composite shape.

How many of the shapes did he put together to make this big shape?

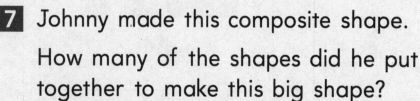

_____

46

1 Which shapes show equal shares?

Circle the **2** correct shapes.

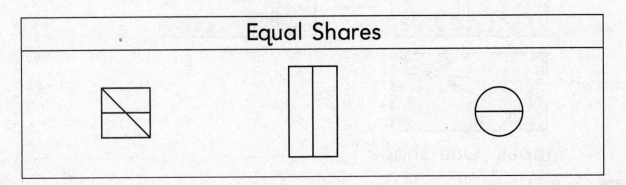

2 Which shows a quarter shaded?

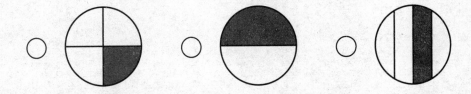

3 Which shapes show halves?

Circle the **2** correct shapes.

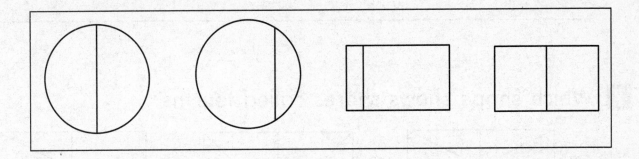

Name _____

4 Which picture shows shares called halves?

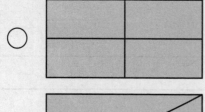 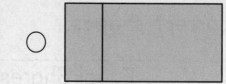

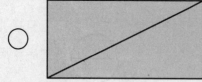

5 Marvin cut his cracker into quarters. Which of these is Marvin's cracker?

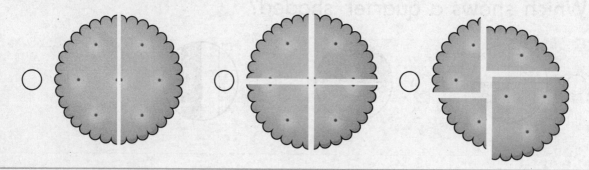

6 How many pieces will there be when a piece of paper is cut in half?

_____

7 Which shape shows shares called fourths?

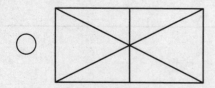 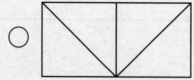 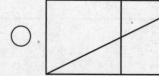

Practice Test

Item	Content Focus	DOK	Record
1	Relate counting to addition and subtraction.	2	
2	Understand subtraction as an unknown-addend problem.	2	
3	Add and subtract within 20.	2	
4	Order and compare objects by length.	1	
5	Tell and write time in hours and half-hours using analog and digital clocks.	1	
6	Count to 120, starting at any number less than 120.	2	
7	Count to 120, starting at any number less than 120.	2	
8	Understand that the digits of a two-digit number represent tens and ones.	2	
9	Distinguish between defining attributes versus non-defining attributes, and build and draw shapes to possess defining attributes.	2	
10	Compose 2-D or 3-D shapes to create a composite shape.	2	
11	Distinguish between defining attributes versus non-defining attributes, and build and draw shapes to possess defining attributes.	1	
12	Use addition and subtraction within 20 to solve word problems.	2	
13	Apply properties of operations as strategies to add and subtract.	1	
14	Apply properties of operations as strategies to add and subtract.	1	
15	Use addition and subtraction within 20 to solve word problems.	2	
16	Add and subtract within 20.	2	
17	Use addition and subtraction within 20 to solve word problems.	2	
18	Determine the unknown number in an addition or subtraction equation.	2	
19	Determine if equations involving addition and subtraction are true or false.	2	
20	Subtract multiples of 10 from multiples of 10 in the range 10–90.	2	
21	Add within 100.	2	
22	Add within 100.	2	
23	Distinguish between defining attributes versus non-defining attributes, and build and draw shapes to possess defining attributes.	1	
24	Compose 2-D or 3-D shapes to create a composite shape.	1	
25	Partition circles and rectangles into two and four equal shares, and describe the shares using the words halves, fourths, and quarters.	2	

This page intentionally
left blank.

1 Josie has 5 apples. She eats 1. How can Josie count to find how many apples are left?

○ 5, 4

○ 5, 6

○ 4, 5, 6

2 Which related addition fact can help solve 13 − 6?

○ 7 + 6 = 13

○ 4 + 9 = 13

○ 3 + 6 = 9

3 Which shows how to make a ten to solve 15 − 7?

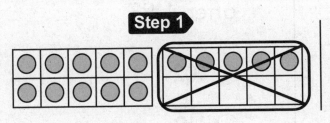 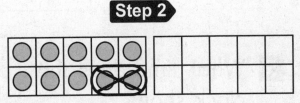

○ 10 − 5 − 2

○ 15 − 5 − 2

○ 15 − 5 − 8

4 Which shows the pencils in order from SHORTEST on the top to LONGEST on the bottom?

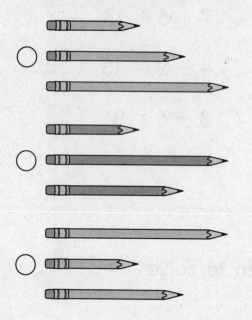

5 What time does the clock show?

○ 6:00

○ 5:30

○ 5:00

6 Count by ones. What numbers are missing?

27, 28, 29, ___, ___, 32

○ 30, 31

○ 33, 34

○ 40, 41

7 Count by ones. What number comes next after 119?

○ 102

○ 110

○ 120

8 What number does this model show?

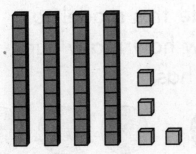

○ 46

○ 47

○ 64

9 How many flat surfaces does a cylinder have?

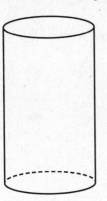

○ 0

○ 1

○ 2

10 Shyam combines these shapes.

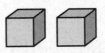

What new shape can Shyam make?

○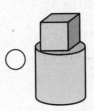

○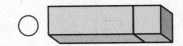

○

11 Which flat surface does a cone have?

○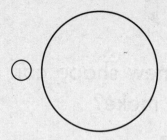

○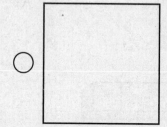

○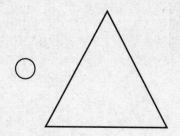

12 Mary has 2 tall cups and 5 short cups. She made this model to show how many cups she has.

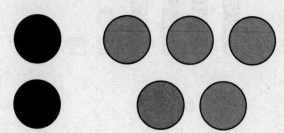

How many cups does Mary have?

○ 3

○ 7

○ 8

13 What is $0 + 3$?

◯ 0

◯ 3

◯ 4

14 Which of these means the same as $1 + 4$?

◯ $1 + 3$

◯ $4 - 1$

◯ $4 + 1$

15 Jill has 6 pennies in her hand. She puts some of the pennies in her pocket. Now she has 2 pennies in her hand. Which equation shows a way to find how many pennies Jill put in her pocket?

◯ ▢ $= 2 - 6$

◯ ▢ $= 6 + 2$

◯ ▢ $= 6 - 2$

16 Which subtraction can be solved using $5 + 9 = 14$?

○ $5 - 9 = \boxed{}$

○ $9 - 5 = \boxed{}$

○ $14 - 9 = \boxed{}$

17 Terry eats 8 crackers. Noor eats 5 more crackers than Terry. Which equation shows how many crackers Noor eats?

○ $8 - 5 = 3$

○ $8 + 5 = 13$

○ $8 + 5 + 5 = 18$

18 What number makes both equations true?

$12 - 8 = \boxed{}$

$8 + \boxed{} = 12$

○ 3

○ 4

○ 6

19 What number makes this equation true?

$11 - 2 = 5 + \underline{}$

○ 4

○ 9

○ 14

20 What is 50 − 20?

○ 3

○ 30

○ 40

21 What is 28 + 6?

○ 24

○ 34

○ 88

22 How many tens and ones are in the sum of these numbers?

$$\begin{array}{r} 45 \\ + 31 \\ \hline \end{array}$$

○ 6 tens and 7 ones

○ 7 tens and 6 ones

○ 8 tens and 6 ones

23 How many vertices does a triangle have?

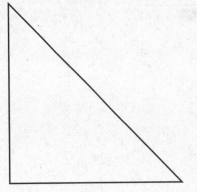

○ 3

○ 4

○ 5

24 Look at this shape.

What parts were combined to make the shape?

○

○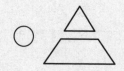

○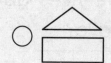

25 Which shows fourths?

○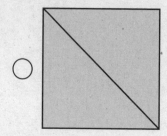

○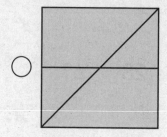

○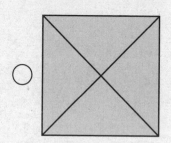

1 Paco had 7 pencils. He gave 2 away. How can Paco count to find how many pencils he has left?

○ 7, 8, 9

○ 7, 6, 5

○ 6, 7, 8

2 Which related addition fact can help solve 11 − 7?

○ 7 + 5 = 12

○ 7 + 4 = 11

○ 3 + 4 = 7

3 Which shows how to make a ten to solve 13 − 6?

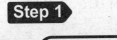 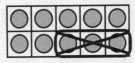

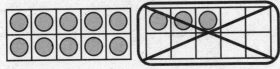

○ 10 − 3 − 3

○ 13 − 3 − 7

○ 13 − 3 − 3

4 Which shows the arrows in order from SHORTEST on the top to LONGEST on the bottom?

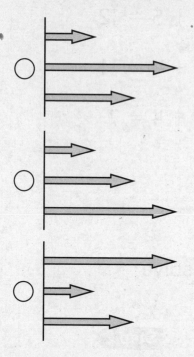

5 What time does the clock show?

○ 12:30

○ 1:00

○ 1:30

6 Count by ones. What numbers are missing?

32, 33, 34, ___, ___, 37

○ 35, 36

○ 38, 39

○ 45, 46

7 Count by ones. What number comes next after 110?

○ 100

○ 101

○ 111

8 What number does this model show?

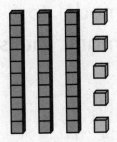

- ○ 34
- ○ 35
- ○ 53

9 How many flat surfaces does a rectangular prism have?

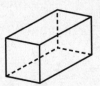

- ○ 0
- ○ 1
- ○ 6

10 Jay combines these shapes.

What new shape can Jay make?

- ○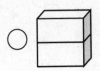
- ○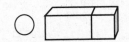
- ○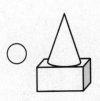

11 Which flat surface does a cube have?

○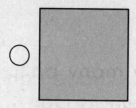

○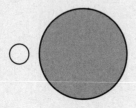

○

12 Lilly has 3 large shells and 6 small shells. She made this model to show how many shells she has.

How many shells does Lilly have?

○ 3

○ 9

○ 10

13 What is 8 + 0?

○ 0

○ 8

○ 9

14 Which of these means the same as 5 + 2?

○ 2 + 5

○ 2 + 3

○ 5 − 2

15 Clare had 6 balloons. She gave some balloons to Dan. Now Clare has 4 balloons. Which equation shows a way to find how many balloons Clare gave to Dan?

○ ▢ = 6 + 4

○ ▢ = 6 − 4

○ ▢ = 4 − 6

16 Which subtraction can be solved using $4 + 8 = 12$?

○ $4 - 8 = $ ▢

○ $8 - 4 = $ ▢

○ $12 - 8 = $ ▢

17 Sam sees 5 ducks. Tara sees 6 more ducks than Sam. Which equation shows how many ducks Tara sees?

○ $6 - 5 = 1$

○ $5 + 6 = 11$

○ $5 + 5 + 6 = 16$

18 What number makes both equations true?

$13 - 7 = $ ▢

$7 + $ ▢ $ = 13$

○ 4

○ 6

○ 7

19 What number makes this equation true?

$5 + 3 = 10 - $ _____

○ 2

○ 8

○ 18

20 What is 80 − 30?

○ 5

○ 40

○ 50

21 What is 39 + 2?

○ 31

○ 41

○ 59

22 How many tens and ones are in the sum of these numbers?

$$53$$
$$+26$$

○ 3 tens and 3 ones

○ 7 tens and 6 ones

○ 7 tens and 9 ones

23 How many vertices does a hexagon have?

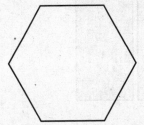

○ 6

○ 5

○ 4

24 Look at this shape.

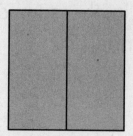

What parts were combined to make the shape?

○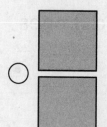

○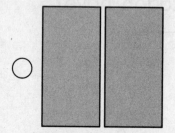

○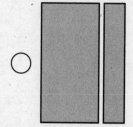

25 Which shows fourths?

○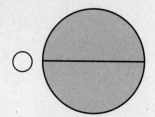

○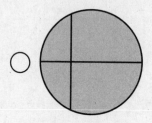

○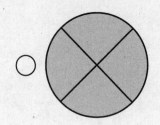

1 Kim has 4 grapes. She eats 3. How can Kim count to find how many grapes she has left?

○ 4, 5, 6, 7

○ 4, 3, 2, 1

○ 3, 4, 5

2 Which related addition fact can help solve 17 − 9?

○ 7 + 2 = 9

○ 9 + 10 = 19

○ 9 + 8 = 17

3 Which shows how to make a ten to solve 13 − 4?

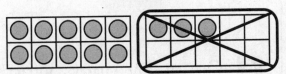 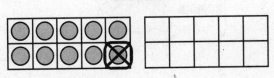

○ 10 − 3 − 1

○ 13 − 3 − 1

○ 13 − 3 − 9

4 Which shows the strings in order from LONGEST on the top to SHORTEST on the bottom?

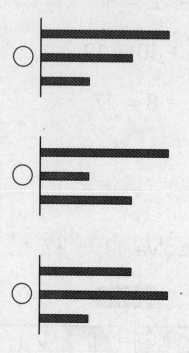

5 What time does the clock show?

○ 7:30

○ 6:30

○ 6:00

6 Count by ones. What numbers are missing?

45, 46, 47, ___, ___, 50

○ 48, 49

○ 51, 52

○ 58, 59

7 Count by ones. What number comes next after 109?

○ 100

○ 101

○ 110

9 How many flat surfaces does a sphere have?

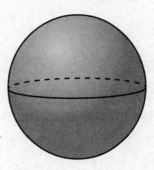

○ 0   ○ 1   ○ 2

8 What number does this model show?

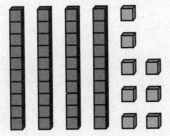

○ 45

○ 48

○ 84

10 Jen combines these shapes.

What new shape can Jen make?

○

○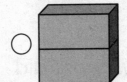

○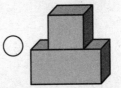

11 Which flat surface does a rectangular prism have?

○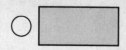

○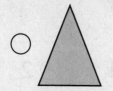

○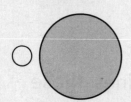

12 Jack saw 4 brown bears and 5 black bears. He made this model to show how many bears he saw.

How many bears did Jack see?

○ 1   ○ 8   ○ 9

13 What is 0 + 7?

○ 0

○ 7

○ 8

14 Which of these means the same as 2 + 8?

○ 2 + 6

○ 8 − 2

○ 8 + 2

15 Nora has 8 crayons in her box. She put some of the crayons on her desk. Now Nora has 3 crayons in her box. Which equation shows a way to find how many crayons are on Nora's desk?

○ $\boxed{} = 3 - 8$

○ $\boxed{} = 8 - 3$

○ $\boxed{} = 8 + 3$

16 Which subtraction can be solved using $7 + 5 = 12$?

○ $5 - 7$

○ $7 - 5$

○ $12 - 7$

17 Owen finds 9 shells. Anna finds 5 more shells than Owen. Which equation shows how many shells Ana finds?

○ $9 - 5 = 4$

○ $9 + 5 = 14$

○ $9 + 5 + 5 = 19$

18 What number makes both equations true?

$11 - 4 = \boxed{}$

$4 + \boxed{} = 11$

○ 3

○ 7

○ 8

19 What number makes this equation true?

$$12 - 3 = 7 + \underline{}$$

○ 2

○ 9

○ 16

20 What is 90 − 50?

○ 4

○ 30

○ 40

21 What is 49 + 3?

○ 42

○ 52

○ 79

22 How many tens and ones are in the sum of these numbers?

$$\begin{array}{r} 45 \\ +22 \\ \hline \end{array}$$

○ 6 tens and 7 ones

○ 6 tens and 3 ones

○ 7 tens and 6 ones

23 How many vertices does a trapezoid have?

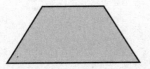

○ 3

○ 4

○ 5

24 Look at this shape.

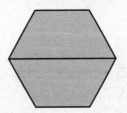

What parts were combined to make the shape?

○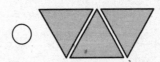

○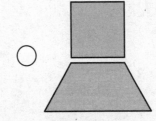

○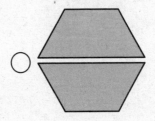

25 Which shows fourths?

○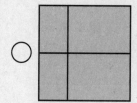

○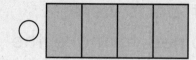

○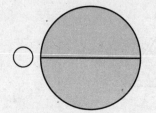